Fat to Soap

B.J. Best

Cavendish
Square

New York

Published in 2017 by Cavendish Square Publishing, LLC
243 5th Avenue, Suite 136, New York, NY 10016

Website: cavendishsq.com

This publication represents the opinions and views of the author based on his or her personal experience, knowledge, and research. The information in this book serves as a general guide only. The author and publisher have used their best efforts in preparing this book and disclaim liability rising directly or indirectly from the use and application of this book.

CPSIA Compliance Information: Batch #CW17CSQ

All websites were available and accurate when this book was sent to press.

Library of Congress Cataloging-in-Publication Data

Names: Best, B. J., 1976- author.
Title: Fat to soap / B.J. Best.
Description: New York : Cavendish Square Publishing, [2017] | Series: How it is made
Identifiers: LCCN 2016026016 (print) | LCCN 2016026737 (ebook) | ISBN 9781502621221 (pbk.) | ISBN 9781502621238 (6 pack) | ISBN 9781502621245 (library bound) | ISBN 9781502621252 (ebook)
Subjects: LCSH: Soap--Juvenile literature.
Classification: LCC TP991 .B435 2017 (print) | LCC TP991 (ebook) | DDC 668--dc23
LC record available at https://lccn.loc.gov/2016026016

Editorial Director: David McNamara
Copy Editor: Rebecca Rohan
Associate Art Director: Amy Greenan
Designer: Alan Sliwinski
Production Coordinator: Karol Szymczuk
Photo Research: J8 Media

The photographs in this book are used by permission and through the courtesy of: Cover (left) D and S Photographic Services/Shutterstock.com, (right) Mark Lund/Getty Images; p. 5 Library of Congress; p. 7 Jade Albert Studio, Inc./Getty Images; p. 9 Alexander Raths/Shutterstock.com; p.11 PHB.cz (Richard Semik)/Shutterstock.com; p. 13 Teodora D/Shutterstock.com; p. 15 Rifkhas/Shutterstock.com; p. 17 Valery Sharifulin/TASS/Getty Images; p. 19 Gary Ombler/Getty Images; p. 21 ©Tim Graham/Alamy Stock Photo.

Printed in the United States of America

Contents

Soap has been used for more than 2,000 years.

Soap cleans many things.

It cleans cars.

It cleans windows.

Soap cleans people.

Using soap helps kill germs.

9

Soap is made with fat.

It can be animal fat.

This fat comes from meat or **dairy** products.

11

Soap can be made with vegetable oil.

This oil is a type of fat.

13

Lye is used to make soap.

Lye is made from **ashes** of burned wood.

Water is mixed with the ashes.

15

Lye is very strong.

It is mixed with warm fat
in a **vat**.

The mixture is like pudding.

The mixture is poured into **molds**.

It cools and hardens.

19

The soap is cut into bars.

It is packaged.

It is ready to clean!

PATOUNIS

reen Olive Soap
h yet friendly cleansing
top to toe use

Ingredients: ...ium hydroxide, ...omace oil saponified with
...er, sea salt. No additives.
www.pa ounis.gr

PAT...
Gree...
Thoroug...

KERKYRA

New Words

ashes (ASH-ez) Small bits left over from a fire.

dairy (DARE-ee) From a farm with cows.

lye (LIE) A strong liquid made from ashes.

mold (MOLD) A shape where a liquid can be poured.

vat (VAT) A large tub.

Index

23

About the Author

B.J. Best lives in Wisconsin with his wife and son. He has written several other books for children. He uses soap.

About BOOKWORMS

Bookworms help independent readers gain reading confidence through high-frequency words, simple sentences, and strong picture/text support. Each book explores a concept that helps children relate what they read to the world they live in.